LOVE OF COUNTRY:

A DISCOURSE,

Delivered on Thanksgiving Day, December 12th, 1850,

IN THE

BLEECKER STREET CHURCH.

BY

THOMAS H. SKINNER,

PROFESSOR IN THE UNION THEOLOGICAL SEMINARY.

NEW YORK:

E. FRENCH, 135 NASSAU STREET.

1851.

S. W. BENEDICT,
Printer, 16 Spruce-Street.

REV. THOMAS H. SKINNER, D.D.:

DEAR SIR,—The undersigned, members of the Bleecker Street Congregation, who had the pleasure of listening to your discourse on *Christian Patriotism*, delivered on the annual Thanksgiving Day, believing it well adapted to promote the best interests of our Country, respectfully request a copy for publication.

We are, dear sir, very truly yours,

JAS. C. BLISS,
MARCUS WILBUR,
WALTER EDWARDS,
WM. A. WHEELER,
E. J. WOOLSEY,
ALFRED C. POST,
E. FRENCH.

NEW YORK, *December* 13, 1850.

TO DR. JAMES C. BLISS, MARCUS WILBUR, ESQ., and others:

GENTLEMEN,—Although the discourse to which you refer, was written some years ago, I trust that its teaching is sufficiently suitable to the times, to justify my consenting to its publication according to your request. I therefore submit it to your disposal. A few paragraphs have been added to it since its delivery, but I do not think they would have varied your opinion as to its character on the whole.

With great regard,

THOMAS H. SKINNER.

January 9th, 1851.

DISCOURSE.

PSALM cxxxvii. 5, 6. If I forget thee, O Jerusalem, let my right hand forget her cunning: If I do not remember thee, let my tongue cleave to the roof of my mouth: If I prefer not Jerusalem above my chief joy.

THESE words, taken from one of the most beautiful and touching melodies ever written even under inspiration, are an effusion of religious patriotism. They were prompted by an insult to that sentiment offered to captive Jews by their oppressors. "They that carried us away captive, required us to sing them one of the songs of Zion: How shall we sing the Lord's song in a strange land? The solemn chant would imply insensibility in us, to the dishonor of our country;—the Holy Land, with all its sacred associations, now lying desolate under the tyrannous hand of our heathen masters. No song of Zion from us shall entertain the ears of profane men, *by the river of Babylon.* Sooner may the divine judgment deprive us of every use both of hand and tongue."

These Jews, in their exile, had not renounced THE LOVE OF COUNTRY: it was stronger in them than the love of life. Was not the affection virtuous? And has not the Holy Spirit, in this inspired Ode, set to it the seal of the Divine approbation?

It has been said that Christianity is against Patriotism: It removes the walls of partition between the different nations; makes the world one brotherhood; and thus leaves no place for the *love of country*, which is a sectarian and selfish sentiment, and is consistent with enmity to mankind. "Patriotism, that celebrated virtue, so much practiced in ancient, and so much professed in modern times, that virtue which so long preserved the liberties of Greece, and exalted Rome to the empire of the world; this celebrated virtue," says a writer on the Evidences of Christianity,* "must be excluded; because it not only falls short of, but directly counteracts the extensive benevolence of this religion." This, I shall, in the first place, show to be an error, or prove that Patriotism is a Christian virtue. Then, secondly, I shall specify the prominent duties of Christian patriotism; and, finally, I shall consider how love to our country, guided by the Gospel, will show itself in reference to two or three subjects of national moment, now exciting special interest, and one of them no small solicitude, amongst us.—

I. It has been erroneously affirmed that the ethics of Christianity deny Patriotism a place among the virtues. Although there is no specific inculcation of it in the New Testament, it should not be hence inferred that the Gospel either disowns or underrates it as one of the modifications of that love which is the fulfilling of the Law. There were sufficient reasons for the silence which was observed on this subject, in the days of our Lord and his Apostles. The Jews were now in a state of vassalage to Rome, and appeals to the love of country, in their circumstances, would have been understood by them as a summons to rebellion against

* Soame Jenyns.

the established government; and had Christianity made such appeals, it would have taught disobedience to one of its own precepts—that which demands submission to the established authorities.—Again, this unhappy people were at this time, the subjects of a fanaticism which made them think malignity toward other nations a duty; and addresses to patriotism would, in their case have been in effect, only exciting and confirming an already rancorous hatred of mankind.—But more than all, this sinful nation, whose history from the beginning had been little else than a record of unparalleled perverseness, had only to perpetrate the murder of Christ in order to fill the measure of their guilt, and bring on themselves those visitations of the Divine wrath by which their political existence was destroyed: and our Saviour, who was well aware of the gathering of the storm, and of the desolation it would produce, was too deeply moved with compassion, to be instilling lessons of patriotism into their hearts, while everything in their condition demanded alarms and calls to repentance.

The time moreover had arrived when the dispensation of Liberty was about to supersede that of Restraint, and all nations in respect of religious rights were to be made equal. The middle wall of separation between Jews and Gentiles was in the process of demolition; and exhortations to the love of country, either in the one or the other, would have had no other tendency, than to engender mutual antipathies, and thus prevent the accomplishment of the gracious design. But the silence of Christianity on that topic, at such a time, no more implied hostility or indifference to patriotism, universally and absolutely, than our being silent about intemperance, on a sacramental occasion, supposes us indifferent to the guilt of that sin.

The Gospel indeed proclaims peace and good-will to the

world: It seeks to make all men in reference to earth, pilgrims and strangers, to unite them in one holy and happy fellowship, and to subject them to new and celestial relationships, strong and lasting as eternity, and embracing in their wide scope, the entire universe of the good, both on earth and in heaven. But the reasoning which would hence infer any inconsistency in the spirit of the Gospel, with the highest degrees of devotion to the welfare of our country, would make Christianity subversive of the foundations of society, and opposed not to nationality only, but to the continuance of the human race: For if the love of country be excluded by the predominance of that heavenly-mindedness which the Gospel inculcates, so are the love of neighborhood, and the love of domestic relations, and all the endearments of friendship, and all local attachments, and the pursuits of business, and labors for a household provision, and whatever else is necessary to the continued existence of man in this world.

It is admitted that Philanthropy, and not Patriotism, is the comprehensive expression, the most complete exponent, of the spirit of the Gospel, in reference to mankind. But there may be expansion without inconsistence; and there may be limitations and degrees, and various forms of interest and affection, connected with the most perfect harmony and unity of spirit. A Philanthropy which has no particular localities, no definite spheres of labor, no fixedness of regards, no specific tasks, no preferences, no individual or vicinal trials and pleasures, is a mere abstraction; why then may not the love of country consist with, nay, be a modification of *the love of Man!* Nothing is more manifest than that the same Law of Nature, which unites us in different degrees of affection, with different portions and individuals of our kind, must originate a peculiar love of country, in every unperverted heart; and therefore to make the spirit of Christianity opposed to patriotism is to make it unnatural.

There is a species of patriotism, so called, which the Gospel does not approve. It was the maxim of Themistocles, that *whatever is advantageous to one's country is just.*—But as that self-love is criminal which pursues its purpose in violation of another's rights, so is that love of country, if it must be so termed, which wantonly interferes with the peace and independence of other nations. Christianity has no encouragement for the darings, no sympathy with the spirit, of an Alexander or a Napoleon, or of any one of the great conquerors, whose exploits history has recorded, or poetry sung; on the contrary, language cannot express its hostility to all, whether individuals or nations, who encroach on the peace and liberty and unalienable rights of others, to aggrandize themselves. A plundering army is in the sight of God, but an association of robbers and murderers, whose individual liabilities will not be alleviated in the day of judgment, because they were banded together and headed by a brave and skillful chief. The triumphs of the Roman Generals which filled the Imperial city with exultation, moved Heaven with purposes of exterminating wrath against the nation.

The religion of Christ is also opposed to the vaunted patriotism of the spirit of party. The Gospel obliges us to seek the Country's good: not the success of one portion of the community in opposition to another. It may be that the interests of the party and of the Country are identical; in which case, while Christianity requires us to pursue those interests, it forbids our doing so with the feelings of rivalry; and if we disregard the prohibition, however successful we may be, it denies us the praise of love to the nation. Good may come to the Country by our means, but our condemnation will be just, unless an honest zeal for the nation's happiness, not the party's triumph, be the motive of our conduct.

II. I proceed to specify the leading Duties embraced in the Love of Country.

1. It has been questioned whether Christians, and especially Ministers of the Gospel, should not stand aloof from all political contests, and either not vote at elections, or conceal their votes, so that their preference among rival candidates for office shall not be known. But is it not a purely selfish and time-serving prudence which ordinarily suggests this course? There may be rare occasions when reserve may be demanded; and our moderation and equanimity in political affairs should always be exemplary; but the cause of our Country is in all respects too important, and especially too closely connected with the interests of religion, to permit any one who is controlled by principle and the spirit of the Gospel, to be in common cases, either negative or unknown in the influence which he exerts. Shall the interests of the nation be abandoned to the blind and headlong action of partisan zeal? When the State, as with us, deprives no man of the elective franchise, no man should deprive himself of it; and if public sentiment is any where opposed to a Clergyman in the calm and regular exercise of this privilege, he ought therein to be opposed to public sentiment; showing that he loves his Country and his Saviour too well, and is too sensible of his final responsibility to God, to consent to the constant disuse of any talent which has been put into his hands.

2. A Patriotism governed by the precepts of the Gospel, cannot be *revolutionary*, so long as the government is ad-

ministered according to legitimate authority, or the commission granted by the laws. We may frankly express our opinions of cabinet measures and legislative enactments. Under our responsibility to God, we should examine and judge whether the executive Head of the nation and all subordinate officers, act in their respective stations with or without authority; and if the limits of power are transgressed by them, we are not bound to silent submission. Circumstances may make it certain that resistance would be unavailing, in which case it would be unjustifiable; but to maintain that non-resistance is universally our duty, is to place God on the side of absolute tyranny, and to deny the *permanent* obligation of Patriotism, unless it be the invariable fact, that magistrates, do what they may, should be left unmolested. But so long as the government which is administered, is that which has been established, and so long as the administration is constitutional on the whole, however imperfect in some particulars, the spirit and the proceedings of Christian Patriotism will be *anti-revolutionary;* and while it may regret and freely censure "the want of wisdom," firmness, clemency and principle in "the powers that be," will not only obey, but sustain, if need be with arms, those duly constituted powers, against all rival ones, foreign or domestic; and this it will do from regard at once to the Country's welfare and the will of God, who has declared the established authorities to be his own ministers, and those who resist them to be adversaries to his ordinance.

3. Nevertheless, Patriotism, as I have intended to assert, may possibly not only consist with, but be active and prominent in promoting Resistance. The noblest manifestations of the love of country have been made in revolutionary conflicts. When magistrates, for their own aggrandizement, maltreat

and oppress the people in the exercise of usurped authority, they are the greatest of criminals, and if there be no appointed means for displacing them, other effectual means, if there be such, should be taken. The same principle in morals, which justifies a man in slaying one who would murder him, gives a people a right to use violent resistance against tyrants whom they cannot otherwise remove. Patriotism in such cases, true to itself as devoted to the national happiness, takes counsel of Expediency, and does not act without regard to probability as to consequences. The question first to be settled is, whether a revolution is practicable; and when no doubt remains on that point, another question demands solution, namely—whether the evils, present and future, incidental to a revolutionary contest, will be less than those which call for a revolution. If resistance would on the whole certainly tend to the nation's damage, to attempt it would be the part, not of patriotism, but of fanatical rashness; and in the sight of God and man would be sedition and treason.

In uncertainty as to duty, we cannot, without folly, disregard the probable consequences of a proposed course of action. It is willful self-murder to expose ourselves to ruin, and worse, if others are to be associated with us, unless we proceed under a firm conviction of the propriety of the measure. Right is to be always done; *fiat justitia ruat cœlum;* but let right be first ascertained. If Heaven is to be overturned, let it not be done by a *mistake*. In ordinary circumstances, right, *justitia*, requires submission "to the powers that be;" and if it sometimes requires or permits resistance to them, it is when the evils which call for resistance are greater than any which may probably connect themselves directly or remotely with revolutionary measures. Right will never be found on the side of those who pursue a course which, on the whole, is against the public good.

It is impossible to detail beforehand the circumstances in which Resistance becomes proper, or to define the limits to which oppression may proceed, before it should be attempted, or to specify the primary or other particular steps to be taken, after it has been resolved upon. The path of Patriotism, first and last, will be discovered and pursued by applying the principle of Expediency to the circumstances that justify or demand resistance. Patriotism resisting the civil authorities, is as thoughtful and reflective, as wise and sedate, as self-renouncing and profoundly studious of the national happiness, as it is sublimely venturous and bold. Resistance is the part, either of the most heroic and exalted form of virtue, or of the most enormous criminality. No responsibility is greater than that which Patriotism assumes when it seeks to subvert unjust and tyrannical rule. To take this responsibility in haste is not the part of patriots but of desperadoes and infatuated fanatics.

4. It is said that Christianity forbids the use of arms—and every form of war, so that *martial courage* is no form of true Patriotism. This, which is manifestly inconsistent with what we have just been propounding, is not the true teaching of Christianity. Though the Gospel would beat swords into ploughshares, and spears into pruning hooks, and keep the world in perfect peace, and though it employs a tone and emphasis of teaching against wars and fightings, which makes the responsibility for them fearful, yet it gives no ground for the conclusion, that it is unlawful to serve one's Country in the camp or the battle-field. When we consider what is written concerning the four Centurions;* and

* Mat. viii. 5 *et seq.*, Luke xxiii. 47, Acts x. 1–8, and xxvii. 11.

the advice of John to the soldiers;† and that the principle which so expounds the scriptures in question, as to draw from them testimony against arms, has not its limit in that inference, but equally condemns all punishment of crime, and either takes the sword from the Magistrate, or makes him bear it in vain, if it does not go against government itself, we find ourselves obliged to protest against this interpretation of the Gospel, as in the highest degree fanatical. Great as are the horrors of war, the same principle which vindicates the Divine Government in permitting these and greater evils, namely—that the highest good of the whole must be maintained against all opposers, at whatever hazards or consequences, vindicates the use of weapons of war in support of the government legally administered, against all assailants from without or within.

5. The spirit of true Patriotism, as we have before said, is one with that of all just government in seeking as its last end the Public Good: and because this is not to be identified with increase in numbers, wealth, territory, or magnificence, but with intelligence and virtue,—the only ground of solid and lasting happiness; and because these are to be permanently secured only by the prevalence of Religion; therefore, while an enlightened love of country must zealously promote the EDUCATION OF THE PEOPLE, it must, while pursuing this object, be mainly intent on their EVANGELIZATION. They are the nation's best friends, who, by holy living, and missionary labors and sacrifices, are infusing the leaven of the gospel into the community. In this Country, the State cannot use the public treasure in advancing Christianity, but that every statesman, judge and ruler should be a Christian in all his conduct, private and official, and

† Luke iii. 14

particularly should be a liberal and zealous patron of Home Missions, is demanded alike by patriotism and religion.

6. One of the greatest duties that we owe our Country, is Prayer for those who are in authority over it. In their hands lie the springs of the national welfare, and they cannot be touched without consequences of good or evil to every interest, civil and spiritual, throughout the whole land. There is not a village, church, family or individual whose interests are not committed to the Country's Head and Council ; and though the Christian's life be hid with Christ in God, and though the final triumph of the Church be certain, it is presumption to expect that the happiness of either country, church or individual is safe, if importunate prayer be not continually offered on behalf of those who bear the burden and responsibilities connected with the administration of the government. If they are wise and holy men, they ought to be prayed for, and much more if they are not. A distinct and prominent place should be given them in the devout exercises of the sanctuary ; nor should it content any one in this high matter to unite with others in public prayer, however solemnly and constantly ; the most earnest supplications for them should ascend daily from every Christian in his closet, and every Christian family in their domestic worship.

7. Finally, though the Church in this land be separate from the State, there is no power which can be brought into action in favor of the nation's happiness, equal to that of the Pulpit. The energies of this Divine means of every good to man, are greatly increased with us, by its disconnection from all civil advantages and aids. If it receive no support, it is under no specific obligations. If it stands alone, it stands independent and free: while there is no place near or remote, no person high or low, no subject

whether of politics, legislation, morals, religion, science or art, to which it may not boldly apply its appropriate influence, under protection of the government, so long as it violates no one's civil rights. This privilege has the American Pulpit. Its field is boundless, its way unobstructed; it may make a full experiment of its powers, and if it does this, the proof will not be wanting to the country, that the Gospel ministry is the best friend to all human interests, national and individual; the State will reverence and cherish, though it cannot espouse, the Church; and the peace of our rising and spreading Republic, will flow as a river, and its righteousness as the waves of the sea.

The Pulpit is often charged with occupying a sphere not its own, and there teaching *against* the Gospel, in its strictures on civil and political matters. Since ministers of the Gospel are of like passions with other men, they have, doubtless, sometimes given occasion for this grave accusation. But if they earnestly endeavor to meet their responsibilities in relation to the matters in question, the most blameless and exemplary manner of doing this, might be no security against the imputation of profaning the pulpit by intermeddling with politics. Ministers of the Gospel are not to hold themselves aloof from observing or criticising the doings of magistrates and politicians. The kingdom of Christ, though not of this world, is over all kings and kingdoms, and governments of whatsoever kind; and of this kingdom the earthly administrators are Ministers of the Gospel; and if they do not appropriately assert the universal supremacy of its Lord and its laws, there is no unfaithfulness so great as that of which they are guilty. If, for the civil government and good of mankind, the "powers that be" are ordained of God, the Christian ministry are also most sacredly ordained of God, to propound his word and assert his authority to all orders of men, whether in low place or high, in office or not, requiring them in all parts of their conduct, and in every act of life, private or public, to obey the Divine Law. If civil legislatures make laws against the Law of God, or if judges and magistrates perpetrate moral wrong in the administration of the law, or if cabinet proceedings be in open violation of the great principles of moral order and rectitude, the silence of the Christian ministry, in view of such offences against the Sovereign of the Universe, would entitle them to the indignant disapprobation of God and men. Far should it be from the Ministers of Christ "to speak evil of dignities;" they should esteem, and teach all men to esteem CIVIL ORDER, as more precious than life; they should enjoin obedience to the laws—*active* obedience, unless the laws be immoral—and passive, unresisting submission to legal penalties, even though the laws be of this character; but as Christ's anointed ambassadors and representatives, they are to maintain HIS just authority—the authority of Truth and Virtue, the supreme rule of Heaven—over all nations, and all human proceedings and acts. And if, in doing this with the "meekness of wisdom," they incur the reproach of trespassing beyond their proper province, or any other reproach, they will, in due time, exchange this unmerited condemnation for the recompense of suffering for righteousness' sake.

III. We now turn our attention to the more particular topics we promised to remark upon. Of those we had in thought, the first which presents itself is—

1. Popular Education.—We have already intimated the important place which this holds among the objects most deeply involving the national welfare. A people who appoint their own officers should be qualified to judge for themselves, as to the fitness of persons to places; otherwise they

must be in this matter as men walking in the dark. If they have no guide, their appointments will be capricious, and may be absurd; and if they are led by others, the work is but theirs in name; they are but living machines for doing their managers' pleasure. This might be less undesirable if it were certain that the hands they were under would be qualified to manage them, but as the case is, the almost certain fact would be the reverse of this. The conclusion is, that popular government, where the people are ignorant, is but a pretence, and that the government *really* in force is that of demagogues—the worst species of despotism.

It is well, therefore, for our Republic, that the work of educating the common people is engaging so much thought. It is an auspicious omen that all our political parties think and speak alike on this point. No party seems to regard popular ignorance as necessary to its success. But there is one thing as to this matter, in which all do not seem to be of the same mind, namely, that *it is not sufficient simply to* EDUCATE *the people*. This, most certainly, is the truth. Education can but render them intelligent; but simple intelligence in human nature is but as light to lawless men who are pursuing the path of crime and ruin. Knowledge is power, and is it desirable to arm depravity with power? Let the history of demagoguism answer this question. Demagogues in relation to the people they have misled, have ever been intelligent men; and what has been their preeminence over them in other respects, but the preeminence of selfish ambition? Make the people simply intelligent; let conscience in them be seared or perverted; let principle be dead; let selfishness be ascendant, and they do but become by education, as a community of shrewd and crafty dealers, ever eyeing one another, to discover advantages for getting the higher hand. The government now will be administered by corruption; the strong will rule, and their sceptre will be iron, and the oppressed will wait the day to exchange the yoke for the throne and the rod. The demand for virtue in a republic is not less urgent than the demand for knowledge; both demands are to be met. With education religion must be conjoined in just proportion. The heart of the nation must be pure, and to this end Christianity must preside in the schools; and educational training, from the beginning and throughout, must be kept under the control and sway of the Word of God.

As friends to our Country, we cannot but rejoice that the several State Legislatures are giving this subject their attention; nothing deserves more their best counsels, and their liberal provision; but there is cause to tremble as well as rejoice. The question is under discussion, whether the Word of God should be read in our Common Schools? It is strenuously urged against this, that our Government being unsectarian, cannot constitutionally interfere with any one's preferences or opinions on this point. The argument would restrain our legislatures from allowing any connection whatever, of religion, with their proceedings. Were there heathens amongst us, they might complain. Atheists themselves might complain of any legislative measure which was against their convictions or consciences, as to matters of religion. Is it so, that our civil authorities must stand as much aloof from all recognition of God and Christ, in the exercise of their functions, as this argument supposes? If it be, with what fearful interest should we examine on what foundation our institutions are resting, and whether our destiny as a nation is not that which awaits all the nations which refuse to acknowledge the sovereignty of Christ.

This objection to the association of religion with popular education, though not triumphant as yet, and we hope for the honor of our Country it never will be, has its advocates among persons who call themselves Christians, and is not without practical influence in our elections and legislative proceedings; and falling in, as it does with man's native enmity against God, it is well suited to inspire every friend of the Country with pensive thought, bearing as it does with direct force against this main pillar of our Republic, THE UNION OF VIRTUE AND INTELLIGENCE IN THE PEOPLE. If it prevail in our legislative bodies, and the Bible be banished by law from the Common Schools, then as our legislation will be against the government of God, we must look elsewhere for the means of popular education, and implore the Divine Mercy in behalf of the civil powers. We are not to despond. There are other resources at hand. The right and the ability will be left us of educating our children, and others under our influence, as we please. Let all private Christians do what they can; let wealthy Christians maintain schools of their own; let the different Evangelical churches undertake this work; and in their periodical councils, consistories, conventions, conferences, and assemblies, let FREE SCHOOLS for the religious education of youth be as adequately provided for, and as carefully supervised, as missions, or any other matter of denominational concern. Thus let the business proceed, and perhaps the mischief of irreligious legislation will be over-ruled, and be made the occasion of greater good than legislative resources, however ample, and however well appropriated, could have accomplished.

2. The next of these topics is ROMANISM.—This is an element in our social State, which does not combine well with our peculiar institutions. Its ascendency would be our overthrow, as an independent people. It would subject us

to the sway of the Pope, whose kingdom is of this world—not spiritual only. The priests of this superstition are under an oath of allegiance to the Roman pontiff, which binds them to him in such a manner, that they could not, without perjury, stand for our country's independence, in opposition to his will. They intend, if possible, to acquire the control of affairs. They have a plan of operations, and they are conducting it with great diligence, and with admirable adaptation to the spirit of the age and the genius of our people. Its instruments are churches, schools, colleges, theological seminaries, convents, nunneries, orphan asylums—unobjectionable, and the most efficient which could have been chosen. It is forwarded by foreign aid—French, Austrian, and Italian Romanists furnish hundreds of thousands a year, for the promotion of their faith in the United States.

This religion is becoming quite prominent and zealous in our political operations, and would make the impression that in some districts it already holds the balance of power. It is unquestionably advancing with great rapidity. Popish emigrants are arriving daily, and in large numbers. Impossibility alone will prevent the success of this bold, crafty, and pernicious system.

What is to be done? We cannot banish Romanism from our shores. Like Slavery, it has a place amongst us, from which it is no easy work to dislodge it. And should we desire its removal? Patriotism forbids. There were Roman Catholics among the achievers of our freedom, and their descendants are with us, having all the loyalty of their fathers; and there are others, not a few, who would resist their own priesthood with the Pope at their head, in defence of the Republic. Far from us be the wish, that our Catholic population might be expelled. Neither should we seek to prevent or diminish the immigration of Catholics. Our country stands open to the oppressed of all nations, and in the name of humanity so may it always stand. The favor of God would be forfeited by closing our door against any portion of suffering mankind. Nor should we receive them otherwise than with kindness, nor deal with them otherwise than as brethren. They come to us with a religion which we cannot look upon with favor, but they come to improve their condition; and even their undesirable religion recommends them to our philanthropic regard. In all appropriate methods we should strenuously resist the schemes of their priesthood and foreign patrons, for the extension of Romanism in this country; but let us, with open arms, and with warm fellow-feeling, welcome the emigrants, in whatever numbers they may come. Let them come from Ireland, from France, from Germany, from Spain, from Italy—let them come as many as will, and sit down with us under the Tree of Liberty, which God has planted in this land for the weary and afflicted of all nations.

Much may be plausibly said against this on the ground of abstract right, and absolute consistency. There is in Romanism the root of every evil: its tendency is everywhere to demoralize man; and it embraces a civil element which cannot commingle with our nationality as an independent people, and which, fully developed and ascendant, would bring us under the yoke of the worst despotism on earth. This is all true. Nevertheless, in the full view and the probable working of things, and as an experiment, which is to proceed under the influence, moral and civil, now advancing with resistless force and astonishing celerity in this country, we may wisely, prudently, and righteously allow, yea, and encourage the influx of Roman Catholics from every part of the world; and it is, therefore, on the whole, incumbent on us to do so. There would be cause for fear if all other influences were to be in abeyance, and Romanism have nothing adverse to encounter; but none, in the actual circumstances in which it must find itself. The Protestant population is gaining on the Catholic at the rate of more than four hundred thousand a year. The Protestant clergy are eighteen or twenty thousand, and the Catholic eight or ten hundred. The Protestants are not inactive, and it is not probable that they will be. The converts from Romanism are many times more than the converts to it. These facts show no cause for fear. Suppositions may be made which would be startling, if there were reason to think they are to be realities; but, except in the imagination of alarmists, there seems to be no reason for such a conclusion; and in a world like this, where the utmost evidence as to the future course of things, cannot transcend probability, we can scarcely hope for higher security than we have, that Romanism is not to prevail in the United States, but to be ultimately lost in the predominance of a nationality, civil and religious, altogether our own.

3. The remaining topic is SLAVERY. This is becoming a subject of extreme interest in this country. It is moving deeply our religious bodies, entering with great earnestness and with decisive effect into our political contests, and profoundly agitating our national councils. As Christian patriots, we cannot be justified in holding toward it the position of neutrality or indifference. It is not probable that the excitement which has been created will subside without some result of importance to the nation. What course does true patriotism require us to take in regard to it? Let no man content himself with denouncing the excitement as the fruit of fanatical zeal. That cannot be done indiscriminately without casting reproach on not a few of the most excellent

and honored of our citizens, and also without disregard to historic truth. This movement in our nation, unhappily as it has proceeded, in too many instances, is referable to a spirit in the age—an invincible spirit, we trust it will prove to be found—which seeks the universal emancipation of man, which should be resolved into the triumph of Christian truth as its remote cause, and which republican America, as having proclaimed to the world the natural equality of mankind, from the beginning of her independence, cannot, without palpable inconsistency, resist. Slavery as a system, should find advocates every where throughout the whole earth sooner than in this land of freedom. It should, and we hope soon will be, the universal desire that the institution utterly cease. But what to do in regard to it under existing circumstances —what Christians seeking the country's good should do, is the question. And it demands for its solution, if any question ever agitated amongst us has done, the guidance of the wisdom which is from above; *the wisdom which is pure, peaceable, gentle, easy to be entreated, full of mercy and good fruits, without partiality and without hypocrisy.* American slavery, whatever evils it includes or propagates, *has law on its side,* and that, if we are not to renounce Christianity, is a serious fact, neither to be overlooked nor simply condemned and denounced. Christianity, as taught and exemplified by Christ and his apostles, does not permit its disciples, either *individually* or in their *synods,* to resist *directly* the civil power, except where that power forbids the exercise of true religion; and that authorizing slavery simply does not amount to this, the sacred records themselves attest. They do this constructively, not merely by silence as to the evils of slavery in the Roman empire, where its form was worse than it is with us, but by the kind of instruction which it requires Christian teachers to give in reference to the subject; by injunctions of obedience to Christian slaves; and by exacting for them from their Chrstian masters, not instant emancipation under all circumstances, but justice and kindness in the exercise of authority. No inference from hence can be drawn to the dishonor of the Gospel, as though it were friendly to the institution of Slavery; but the just observation is, that the Gospel being designed for the reformation of wrong-doing, and not for its condemnation merely, and relying for its success not upon miracles, but persuasion and the blessing of God, would not defeat its own end by provoking the magistrates' resistance, with no means at hand of staying the devouring sword. The times, it is true, are different, but there is no change with us rendering obsolete or inapplicable the teaching of primitive Christianity on this subject. There is a greater number of the professors of Christianity; its spirit and power in the community are of wider extent; but the State with us holds itself aloof from the Church, and stands as Rome did in defence of Slavery; and we have no want of proof that the tendency of direct aggression upon the object around which its powerful shield is thrown, is to inflame popular and *civil* indignation.

Our wisdom in walking, as to this matter, in the footsteps of the apostles, would appear, from another consideration. If the State interposed no obstacle; if it were convinced of the impolicy of Slavery, and desirous of bringing it to an end, and ready to enter upon prudent and feasible measures for its abolition at once, would there be no obstructions to be surmounted, no provisions against incidental evils to be devised, nothing to be done to prepare the slave population for a condition of independence? Is it not morally certain that abrupt legislation against our slavery, would lead to evils in the country scarcely less, on the whole, than the slavery itself, and in respect to slavery be abortive? How unwise, therefore, that a course should be pursued implicating the laws and slaveholders together in atrocious guilt, for not bringing the system to an end in a day! There should be no question as to the intrinsic and enormous evil of Slavery, as existing in this country; but it is a maxim of wisdom and virtue, that *many things which ought not to have been done, are, because they are done, not to be undone.* The institution of American Slavery, we hope in God, is not one of these things. It is, doubtless, in one way or another, sooner or later, to be undone. A tide of opinion and feeling is rising against it, which, if things proceed as they are now doing, will at length become too powerful to be resisted. If, however, it be undone, with advantage to the slaves, and without hazard to the peace of the nation, the result must be effected, not by an impetuous driving home of abstract right and truth, but by the meekness of wisdom operating in the indirect, gentle and suasory methods of primitive evangelism. In this age, and especially in this free land, the discussion of the subject should, as it will, be prosecuted; but this should be done *thoroughly;* the subject should be looked at on all sides; all the difficulties connected with it should be admitted and considered; allowances should be made for circumstances tending to mitigate the country's responsibility, as having had the evil entailed upon it; and the proceedings in regard to it should be marked by exemplary meekness, taking note of the glaring fact, that the materials and causes for excitement in this affair are peculiarly abundant, both in the actors and those to be acted upon. These, so far as we can see, are the general principles by which our love of country should direct its way in relation to this subject.

They are, I think, the proper directory of our patriotism in reference to the excitement now prevailing about the restoration of fugitives from slavery. The immediate occasion of this excitement is a legislative measure for the maintenance of principles of order, which were settled, when the compact was formed, on which the American Union is based. The States originally composing this Union bound themselves by a sacred compact to observe these principles, and the other States also are under the same obligation. These foundations of the Union had been disturbed, and our national Council, after serious and long deliberation, enacted this law as a measure for securing them against further molestation. That it would produce excitement could not but have been foreseen from the existing state of feeling in the country in regard to Slavery; but its justification is, that this, or some other not less efficacious measure, was necessary to prevent a worse evil—the violation of the national compact, tending to the disruption of the bonds of Union, and the overthrow of the great American Republic.

The law has given dissatisfaction on various grounds: It has been thought by some to be unconstitutional, by others to be at least inexpedient, and not a few have denounced it as positively immoral, or against the law of God. Without attempting to examine its character, or interfering with any one's judgment of it in any point of view, the path of Patriotism is manifest. Be the just estimate of the law in question what it may, if such a country as this is any longer an object to be loved or desired, if American Patriotism has not become an unlawful and vicious sentiment, violent resistance to the authorities of the land is one of the highest crimes that man can commit.

It is universally felt that the restoration of fugitives from bondage is, in itself or apart from civil relations and affinities, a work of simple injustice and inhumanity; but where such fugitives themselves are violators of civil order, and where those who oppose their restoration are violators of the same order, and of their own sacred covenant, whereby they have bound themselves not to violate it, no true humanity, or justice, or virtue, in any form, will forcibly resist the execution of a law requiring their restoration. The alternative now is, either to let the law have its course, or to overthrow if possible the government of the country,—and the office of casuistry here, is to judge which of these two will prove the greater evil. If the destruction of the government would be for the advantage of the slaves, would this compensate the evil in which it would involve the interests of the nation and of mankind?

There is no difference as to the course to be taken, whether the law be immoral or not, so far as resisting the government is concerned. Those who think it immoral should not violate conscience, by doing what to them would be wrong, but let them not violate social order and resist the ordinance of God, by refusing to suffer patiently what obedience to conscience may cost them. They have in this country the right of remonstrance and petition, and of using whatever means they may think best, consistently with keeping the public peace, for obtaining the regular repeal of the law; let them, if they choose, avail themselves of their rights; but unless they are convinced that it is their duty to seek the overthrow of the government, they are not more bound in conscience to decline obeying the precept of the law than they should be to bear meekly and unresistingly the infliction of its penalty for their disobedience. Let them love the Constitution of their country well enough to suffer for it patiently, even though they love God and virtue too well to do wrong though at their Country's bidding. To resist the authorities in the regular administration of a law, simply because it is supposed to be unjust, is the part, not of loyalty to God, but of rebellion against both God and the State.

Nor would it vary the character of the resistance, if not a particular enactment only, but the Constitution itself, enjoined as some seem to hold that it does enjoin, the violation of essential morality, in relation to this matter. Whether the Constitution, or a particular law, require wrong-doing, the requirement will be obeyed by no conscientious man; but violently to resist the government on account of immorality in the Constitution, is another and a most flagitious immorality, unless it be justifiable to attempt a revolution on this account. In vain is it alleged that there is a higher law than the Constitution. For the purpose intended, namely, to justify resistance, there is no higher law, unless it be a law which exalts itself above all that is called God, or is worshipped. God has given no law authorising resistance to civil government, when there is no sufficient cause for a revolutionary contest.

In conclusion, let us bear in mind, with grateful wonder and praise, that, while as Christians, the love of country is not only allowed, but required of us by our Holy Religion, we have a country so preeminently deserving of our best affection, our most devoted attachment; a country most remarkably signalized by dispensations of the Divine favor from its beginning; and never more so distinguished than at the present moment; a country the most favored, the most prosperous, and the most happy on the globe; and a country advancing in power and greatness with a rapidity of which the history of nations affords no parallel, and which commands the admiration of the world. How many waters should it require to quench, how many floods to drown the flame of American patriotism. O my Country, with all thy faults, if I forget thee, let my right hand forget her cunning. If I do not remember thee, let my tongue cleave to the roof of my mouth, if I prefer not my Country above my chief joy.

www.ingramcontent.com/pod-product-compliance
Lightning Source LLC
LaVergne TN
LVHW020742120826
845150LV00010B/2355

* 9 7 8 1 4 1 8 1 9 3 7 8 2 *